I AM
SOMEBODY

Embracing the You That **GOD** Created

WILLIE DIGGS

I AM SOMEBODY
Copyright © 2018 Willie Diggs

All rights reserved. Printed in the United States of America. No part of this book may be used or reproduced in any manner whatsoever without written permission except in the case of brief quotations in critical articles or reviews.

Unless otherwise noted, all Bible quotations are from the King James Version of the Bible.

Cover Design, Typesetting, Book Layout by
Enger Lanier Taylor for In Due Season Publishing

Published By: In Due Season Publishing
                Huntsville, Alabama
                indueseasonpublishing@gmail.com

www.indueseasonpublishing.com
ISBN-13: 978-1-970057-00-3
ISBN-10: 1-970057-00-9

            WWW.WillieDiggs.com
        Facebook Search: Willie Diggs
Instagram/Twitter/Periscope: IamWillieDiggs
          Email: jabas03@aol.com

I AM SOMEBODY

Limits of Liability and Disclaimer of Warranty

The author and publisher shall not be liable for your misuse of this material. This book is strictly for informational and educational purposes. The purpose of this book is to educate and entertain. The author and/or publisher do not guarantee that anyone following these techniques, suggestions, tips, ideas, or strategies will become successful. The author and/or publisher shall have neither liability nor responsibility to anyone with respect to any loss or damage caused, or alleged to be caused, directly or indirectly by the information contained in this book.

Views expressed in this book do not necessarily reflect the views of the publisher.

Printed in the United States of America

TABLE OF CONTENTS

DEDICATION 7

ACKNOWLEDGEMENT 8

INTRODUCTION 9

CHAPTER 1 11

CHAPTER 2 18

CHAPTER 3 26

CHAPTER 4 35

CHAPTER 5 43

CHAPTER 6 50

CHAPTER 7 54

CHAPTER 8 68

CHAPTER 9 74

CHAPTER 10 77

Dedication

I dedicate this book to my three sons, Rodelle, Quavonta, and Willie along with my grandson Jayden "Chugs" and granddaughter Jaycee "Shug." I love you all more than words can describe. It is my prayer that you never have to guess what the plans of God are for your life.

Acknowledgments

I would like first to thank God who chose me when people said that I was not worthy. I would like to thank my wife Shataun Diggs who constantly pushes and encourages me in the journey. Honey, thanks for doing life with me!!! I would also like to thank my children Rodelle, Quavonta, and Willie; you guys are my world. I hope that as you watch me grow into who God has said that I am that you look in the mirror of your life and see that you are *somebody* too. Special Thanks to my Aunt Catherine Pickett and Linda Sue Collier, who encouraged me to write and tell my story. I would like to acknowledge my Pastors Superintendent Anthony Wheeler and Sa'Brina Wheeler for your constant love and support. Also to my sister Valerie Diggs and Marsha Deloach for being the best sisters a little brother could have. Special thanks to all of my spiritual children, my mentees, my Beacon Hill Worship Center Family, The Beacon Butler Campus "Squad," and the Diggs, Starks, and Pickett family. You guys Rock!!!!

INTRODUCTION

Am I good enough? Why did it happen to me? Who am I? Am I good for anything? Those are just a few of the many questions that plague our thoughts every day. Have you ever been so lost that finding who you are seems like a dream with no pictures? Questions, questions, and more questions flood our lives to the point that even the questions begin to talk to us. Growing up without my father and losing my mother seemed to push me deeper into confusion about who I was. It was only once I learned the value of mentorship and meeting the Creator (God) that I finally realized who I was because I found out whose I was.

I Am Somebody is a book designed to assist individuals through dialogue to help them gather the evidence needed to prove to themselves that they are a designer's original and that they were not an accident in the laboratory of God. I want the readers to use the tools and tips in this book to grow in their relationship with God and to reevaluate their existence. In the words of Edger A. Guest, "Figure it out for yourself my lad you have all that the greatest of men have had." Let's figure it out together!!!

CHAPTER ONE
I Am a Survivor

Wow, I would have never seen myself in this place. Life for me has been to say the least interesting. Surviving life's tragedies is not an easy task. The tragedies for me started very early in my life. At the age of three to be exact, was the year I experienced my first loss. My father Willie F. Diggs Sr. passed away in a Hospital on Christmas Eve.

A Son's Cry for His Father

Imagine being in a world and left with so many questions and never being able to get the answers. My father was a Staff Sgt. in the military and often traveled and spent several weeks away from us as a family. My memories of him are scattered and a bit confusing. I remember how he looked, his voice tone, and how I felt when he was home. I always felt safe when he was there. I remember the feeling of being secure and protected.

I was only three years old when he died, which left me with a mind full of questions. I remember the relationship he had with my sister Val. She was very close to him, and I remember bits and pieces of my last day with him. We were back in the states from Germany visiting family. My sister explained that we were at home on a family emergency. As we traveled back from what I have always thought was a family vacation, my father became very ill. I remember him throwing up and the look on his face of not feeling well. He made my mom take us back to Germany while he went to the doctor.

My mom argued with him about his decision. However, he managed to talk her into leaving. I remember the kiss he gave her. I will always remember that for the rest of my life. It was certain that they both loved each other. My dad was a very strong-willed individual.

I do not recall a lot about the flight back overseas, but I know it was a long trip. Once we returned home, mom got us settled, and I will never forget the next chain of events for the rest of my life. There was a knock on the door and once my mom answered, she was very anxious and flustered. I remember her crying and packing our clothes up again. She told my sister Val that Fred, whom she often called my dad, was sick and we had to get back to him quickly.

We boarded another plane headed back to the states. My mom was very emotional the whole trip back. Once we arrived at the hospital, my sister and I were excited to see dad. We did not understand what was going on. We just wanted to see him, and then we received heartbreaking news. I remember my mom screaming and crying from what the nurse told her. I did not quite understand what all of the fuss was about. Then my sister Val started crying, calling his name and screaming to the top of her lungs. I want my daddy; I want daddy. She did this repeatedly. She continually called for a person who would never answer. I remember the crying and all of the emotions. Then, my mom told me that my dad had died... I did not understand it. What does that mean? Where is my daddy? Where is my security? Where is my protection? He was gone. My dad was dead. Even worse, it was Christmas. The day that I found out my dad had died was Christmas. Isn't that supposed to be a happy time for kids? The nurse had informed my mom that my dad died Christmas Eve from cancer in the liver and that we arrived 24 hours too late. I grew to know that my dad was a very private person. He did not inform my mom that he had cancer. She had no clue. Later, I found out that cancer hit his body so quickly that he was unable to inform her of what was going on with his health. He had handled everything as it related to final arrangements, how we were going to be taking care of, and how our college tuition would be paid for. Then, he was gone...

<u>Psalm 127:3-5</u>
Sons are a heritage from the LORD, children a reward from him. Like arrows in the hands of a warrior are sons born in one's youth. Blessed is the man whose quiver is full of them. They will not be put to shame when they contend with their enemies in the gate.

    It has taken me 33 years to talk about life without my dad and how to embrace the concept that God does not make mistakes. I have asked the question why me...more than I could possibly count. What I have discovered is that there are some things that I may never fully understand. However, at this stage of my life, I am ok with that. The loss of my father taught me:

1. I am a survivor, and that life will have some unexplainable tragedies, but with God, you can

live through them. There were several times on this journey that I wanted to give up, but because I did not, I am able to tell this story.

2. I learned that when a son is without his father, it is imperative that he gets to know the Father of all of creation. Growing up without my dad to date has been one of the hardest things to deal with in my life. Now, that I know my heavenly Father, I know that I have a purpose and destiny.

3. I learned that on this journey of life I am not alone. When I lost the security of my father at the tender age of three, I often struggled with being secure in life. Was everything going to be ok? Is this thing going to take me out? Will I ever recover from this? The fact that you are reading this book should testify and give reference to the questions above. I am a survivor, and you are a survivor as well.

My Why

Discovering my why in survival mode was not something that came easily to me. After several years of falling and getting back up;

falling and getting back up, and falling and getting back again, I found my why. Your why is that thing that makes your survival valid. My why is my wife and children. Your why may be your nieces, nephews, or your dreams and goals. Whatever it is, find it and allow it to fuel your survival. I think it is imperative that you write your why down so that it is visible to you on a regular bases. There is no right or wrong with your why it is all up to you. Take time today to write down why you must survive. By the way, you are a survivor! I thought I would tell you just in case you have not embraced it yet.

What is that thing that makes you get up in the morning after life's tragedies? That is your why?
_____
_____
_____
_____

What did your tragedy teach you? (Whitney Houston stated in one of her songs, "I didn't know my own strength.")
_____
_____

I AM SOMEBODY

How did what I survive make me better?

Chapter Two
I Am a Seed

Anyone can count the seeds in an apple, but only God can count the number of apples in a seed.
Robert H. Schuller

Loss, loss, loss; years of nothing but loss. I spent several years dealing with the loss of my father, who never got the opportunity to embrace who I was and what I could become. That may be foreign to many, but when you experience major loss in your life and you miss the affirmation of your father, then you have some identity deficits. Now don't get me wrong, I was not always sad, crying, or even depressed, but because of his absence, I did not know who I was.

A Designer's Original

When you think about where you came from you must trace it back further than your parents. Typically, your first point of reference would be your biological parents. For me, I wanted to go a little bit further. I am seed; a designer's original. Before you can figure out the purpose of the seed, you must identify the tree that it came from. Before you can identify the purpose or original intent of the book, you must be informed about the author.

If you know that you are a seed and you are, you must reference your author. For me that is God. Yes, I am, and you are designed by a creator who is amazing. You should take just a couple of minutes to let that sink in. When you realize that you are a designer original, it removes all doubt about you being a mistake. Our God was not in his laboratory experimenting when he created us. We were uniquely designed by a master designer who threaded us together with every gift and talent that we need.

Remember, the type of seed you are is directly related to what type of tree you come from. God, who is our designer, is so powerful and amazing that when He spoke mere words the evidence of His speech manifested. When He spoke, His designs were so magnificent that His words created something from nothing. His words were so creative that even the land and the water separated at His command. That is who your designer is, and if the author of your life is that powerful, then you must understand that you have creative power and that you are powerful in your own right. I love when we look at our God who is described in scripture as, "I Am that I Am." He is such an amazing God. Everything that He made was good!

Affirmation

Currently, one of our biggest struggles is that we are constantly waiting for others to affirm us. The affirmation of others is a powerful thing. However, when you speak words of affirmation over yourself, you really take charge of your life. What is an affirmation? Affirmations are words that encourage or push you to be who or what you desire. For example, I affirm myself daily by reminding myself that I Am Somebody. You get it.... I make sure that if no one else tells me, I tell myself.

Now let me tie something together here. Remember, your Creator has creative ability, and His words are so powerful that when He speaks things happen. Well, I believe that is something that we often forget. The Bible tells us in Proverbs 18:21 that death and life are in the power of the tongue; and those who love it will eat its fruit.

So just to be clear, be very careful of the words that you speak about yourself and the words you allow your peers to speak to you. I often hear young people using their words so carelessly with joking and talking about others. Let's get rid of that type of behavior today. We are too powerful to use our words haphazardly. We need to be direct and intentional when we speak about ourselves or when we speak to others. Below is a simple exercise that will help you with your affirmations. Make them good, direct and intentional. Another tip that I use with affirmations is that I search the Bible to find out what my Creator says about me. Here are just a few.

Psalms 139:14(KJV)
I will praise thee; for I am fearfully and wonderfully made: marvelous are thy works; and that my soul knoweth right well.

What do you think when you read what your Creator said about you?
_____
_____

I AM SOMEBODY

_____
_____
_____
_____
_____

Jeremiah 29:11-13 (KJV)

11 For I know the thoughts that I think toward you, saith the Lord, thoughts of peace, and not of evil, to give you an expected end.

When you read that you have an expected end, I hope that it confirms that you were not a mistake. How does reading this scripture make you feel? It really made me happy. What are your thoughts?

_____
_____
_____
_____
_____

1 Peter 2:9 (KJV)

But ye are a chosen generation, a royal priesthood, an holy nation, a peculiar people; that ye should shew forth the praises of him who hath called you out of darkness into his marvelous light:

Wait...wait...wait... When I read this, it really empowered me and made me think about my friends and myself. Many of you have friends that need to know that your whole generation has a purpose. Write their names down and send them this message. You may even want to tell them to order this book, but at least reach out to them today and encourage them. Take a break after writing their names down, get your phone and start encouraging them.

What do you think when you read what your Creator said about you? We are a powerful group of people.

_____
_____
_____
_____
_____
_____
_____
_____
_____
_____

I AM SOMEBODY

I AM SOMEBODY

Never forget that you are seed that came from a very powerful tree. Use your affirmations to lift you up when you are feeling down. They will help you on this journey called life. Remember what you say about yourself is much more important than what others say about you. So, do not get distracted by the noise of the critics or haters. Stay focused and use your words wisely. You are a seed and the day is coming when the earth will see your fruit.

Chapter Three
I Am Valued

Just because fate doesn't deal you the right cards, it doesn't mean you should give up. It just means you have to play the cards you get to their maximum potential.
Les Brown

    Knowing your worth is the starting point of getting you positioned in the right direction. I was always taught that I had value and that I could be anything that I wanted to be. In this life, you must be willing to face the fact that the way you value yourself will determine how you manage the people around you. I must be honest; although I was raised to value myself, it did not always show up when I made certain decisions. I was lucky to have some cool friends who saw value in me, even when I did not see it in myself. I will never forget when I was young I wanted to join a local gang, but my friends would not let me. I will never forget walking on the railroad track with one of my homeboys as we were going to be jumped in. While on our way, my friend turned to me and told me to go home. He turned and spoke these words to me, and I will never forget what he said. "Satcho, go home, you are different from us." My nickname was Satcho, which all of my friends called me. What my friend was saying was that I had value and that although I wanted to be like everyone else, I was not. My friend had value too; he just did not see it. Although, he went on to join the gang, the fact that he saw so much in me that he did not want me involved in something that would take my value down. Do you have friends that can see the best in you? Do you have friends that will check and correct you when you are wrong? Do you have friends that will not allow you to do things that may put your value at risk?

What About Your Friends?

I often tell my students and mentees that anyone can be a big fish in a small tank. Here is a bit of wisdom; if you are the most popular, intellectual, creative person in your circle, then you are in the wrong circle. A friend is a representation of your future destiny. Their relationship with you will either push you towards your destiny or cause you to abandon it. When you are looking at your circle of friends, you must be honest with yourself. Never allow your comfort zone to be a prison for you. Often times we allow people and their opinions to cause us to take our eyes off our value. I am not saying that you have to be a goodie two shoes, but you must recognize your value so that you can stay on track. When you realize you are of great value, you probably will look at life different. Do not forget that although you may have some life struggles, you are valuable. No mistake you have made or will ever make will take your value away from God. It is my hope that as you read through this chapter, that you really take a good look at your life and see that you are valued and the people that you surround yourself with must see and recognize the value that you have. Let's do some work.

Who are your friends? I want you to write them down because only you know why they are your friends and how you benefit each other.

_____
_____
_____
_____

I AM SOMEBODY

_____
_____
_____
_____

Do your friends know your value? If so, why or why not? This is something that I do even to this day because we must be intentional in our relationships with people.

_____
_____
_____
_____
_____
_____

List your attributes and strengths you have that will benefit your friends.

_____
_____
_____
_____
_____
_____

What are your weaknesses and something that every person who comes in relationship with you needs to know? For example, I am very focused and I do not like to waste my time.

_____
_____
_____
_____
_____
_____
_____
_____

There is a story in the Bible that speaks about the value of a friend. Let's look at this story and build some creditability on the value of friendship.

Mark 2:1-6

*Jesus returned to Capernaum, and a few days later the news went out that He was at home. **2** So many people gathered together that there was no longer room [for them], not even near the door; and Jesus was discussing with them the word [of God]. **3** Then they came, bringing to Him a paralyzed man, who was being carried by four men. **4** When they were unable to get to*

Him because of the crowd, they [a]removed the roof above Jesus; and when they had dug out an opening, they let down the mat on which the paralyzed man was lying. 5 When Jesus saw their [active] faith [springing from confidence in Him], He said to the paralyzed man, "Son, your sins are forgiven."

    This is such an interesting and relevant story. This brother who was a paraplegic, (meaning he had restricted or no movement in his limbs) had to be totally dependent and trust these four guys to carry him into the house of the Savior. Picture this, being totally dependent on others to get you to a place of help. Can you imagine the thoughts, anxiety, or even the shame that could have been present in this story? I marvel at the confidence and value that speaks so loudly in this scripture. These guys had to really value their friend so much that they would pick him up and carry him a distance in an attempt to get him help. To take it further, they also valued him so much that they did not give up on him or the process. No level of fatigue, social, or environmental stress prevented them from helping their friend. They did whatever it took to make sure that he got into that house. They pressed forward, took him to the top of the roof, and began to dismantle the home so that their friend could get some help. Now that is displaying the value of a friend.

Love yourself

Steve Maraboli said, "The most powerful relationship you will ever have is the relationship with yourself." One of the most powerful things that my mother taught me growing up was to "love yourself." I know we live in a world that shuns people who discuss loving themselves as being arrogant and self-centered, but that is not the case for everyone. You must have a healthy sense of love for yourself, or you will devalue your very existence. When people truly start to love themselves, they are great at loving others.

You should be strategic with self-care. I am naturally a giver, as well as some of you. Nevertheless, we must be careful that we aren't so caught up caring for and loving others that we fail to spend time learning and positioning ourselves to grow. How much time are you spending focusing on you? Many people are scared to be alone, hate spending time alone, and never invest in themselves. So today let's make a change to value ourselves and refuse to allow people to misuse, abuse, manipulate, or waste our time. Since we are now getting a better understanding of our values, we should make better use of how we spend our time. I think it is wise to take a day or at least a few times a month and focus on you. Do things that grow you and push you to be better. I hope that this book is something that you will use as a tool to review your self-value. Remember, time is the one thing that you cannot regain. So value the use of your time responsibly.

Now let's deal with some time and value wasters while we are reviewing value. What are you worried about that you cannot change? Write it down and let it go.

_____
_____
_____
_____
_____

We spend too much time trying to fix things that devalue us. Let this book give you permission to let it go and move on. Your destiny is waiting on you, and you cannot afford to waste valuable time chasing something that is dead. When you find your value, you will not focus on the minor things that are intended to throw you off course. Refocus your life in such a way that everything you do from the time you wake up, until the time you lay down is on purpose. Give yourself permission to be free from life clutters. You are somebody, and I am somebody as well!

Chapter Four
I Am Loved

Love is a friendship that has caught fire. It is quiet understanding, mutual confidence, sharing and forgiving. It is loyalty through good and bad times. It settles for less than perfection and makes allowances for human weaknesses.
Ann Landers

Love is not an easy discussion when it comes to the life of the broken. It never ceases to amaze me how we are so quick to repeat and throw around the word love when we have very little understanding of the word. I am not going to attempt to define the word love, but it is my hope that I point you in the direction of understanding its attributes and character. Sometimes some are so heartbroken that they confuse lust with love. Do you love your fellow peers? Do you love your spouse? Do you love your children? Do you love yourself?

It is really difficult to love someone else when

you do not love yourself. As discussed in the previous chapter, we give so much of ourselves away that we forget that self-care is important. Loving yourself enough to take care of your reputation, your soul, and your life is the showcase of people who really love themselves.

I must admit that loving yourself causes you to really look in the mirror and see the real you; the you that is imperfect; the you that has made mistakes; and the you that only you know. When we are in search of love, too many times we wear a false mask so that people will love us. Once the mask falls off, we find ourselves feeling abandoned. So, from this point on, we are living in a mask free zone. From this very second, we are making a commitment to ourselves we will not pretend to be something that we are not. We will accept our flaws, with the desire to change and correct them, and fully embrace the fact that we are fearfully and wonderfully made. Once you remove the mask, you are now open to living in the mask free zone.

Life will cause you to put on a mask and hide. Family dysfunctions, losing a loved one, failed relationships, and peer pressure will make it difficult to remove the mask. Let's take time to discuss why

I AM SOMEBODY

we put on the mask in the first place.

What causes you to hide the real you? What are your fears about being yourself?

_____
_____
_____
_____
_____
_____
_____
_____
_____

What would you do in life if you were not afraid?

_____
_____
_____
_____
_____
_____
_____
_____
_____

    The thing that you wrote down is the thing that fear is robbing you of. I despise a thief. It disturbs me greatly when someone takes things that do not belong to them. Fear is poison to the mind. Be quick to rid yourself of it when it shows up. I find things that contradict fear as a way of fighting it. For example, if I am afraid of being alone, I remind myself that Jesus will never leave me or forsake me; for me, that thought is comforting. So, let's build up our toolbox to combat fear.

Research and write some scriptures (my preference), quotes, or poems that speak against your fears. Feel free to use GOOGLE. Below, list three of your prominent fears and write something that you can do to encourage yourself.

#1 Fear_____

_____
_____
_____
_____
_____
_____
_____
_____
_____

#2 Fear _____

#3 Fear _____

Once people find out who they are, they can position themselves to love and be loved by others. I cannot end this chapter without talking about the day I found *her*; the day I found Shatuan, the love of my life. Interestingly enough, we found each other. I have the most loving wife in the world, and I am not saying that because I am writing a book. You can literally ask anyone who has met her, and they will say the same thing. We have been together for almost 20 years, and she has never said anything bad about another person. She is so quick to forgive and to love. On the other hand, I needed some work in that area. She displays all of the attributes of love. She also has these hugs…. My… my… my…. When she hugs you, it is as if she takes all of your cares away because she is so genuine.

<u>1 Corinthians 13:4-7 (MSG)</u>

***3-7** If I give everything I own to the poor and even go to the stake to be burned as a martyr, but I don't love, I've gotten nowhere. So, no matter what I say, what I believe, and what I do, I'm bankrupt without love.*
Love never gives up.
Love cares more for others than for self.
Love doesn't want what it doesn't have.
Love doesn't strut,
Doesn't have a swelled head,
Doesn't force itself on others,
Isn't always "me first,"
Doesn't fly off the handle,
Doesn't keep score of the sins of others,
Doesn't revel when others grovel,
Takes pleasure in the flowering of truth,
Puts up with anything,
Trusts God always,

*Always looks for the best,
Never looks back,
But keeps going to the end.*

The above scriptures represent what you should expect from the person you desire to be with. These same attributes should be what you bring to the relationship as well. I am not encouraging you to create a checklist, but I really do think that once we embrace the love shown to us from God, then we are in a better position to receive and share His love.

If you are a person that struggles with loving people, I encourage you to take time to pray and ask God to shift your heart. Remember, you are loved, and because of that, you owe humanity that same type of love. Below is a simple prayer that can help keep your heart in the right place.

The Love Prayer

Heavenly Father, thank you for loving me even when I have not loved myself as you have desired. Thank you for loving me so much that you would send your Son just to prove to people like me that we are loved. Help my heart be more like yours. Coach my tongue so that I can have love flowing through my daily conversations. Most of all help me to have a heart like

I AM SOMEBODY

yours; one that forgives easily; constantly serves others, and is faithful to be a friend to all mankind. ~Amen

Chapter Five
I Am Sorry

To forgive is to set a prisoner free and discover that the prisoner was you.
Lewis B. Smedes

One of the most dangerous things that a person can do is to live a life where they deny who they really are. At one point, I did not embrace the "me" that I was created be. Once I began to deal with the skeletons in my own closet, then I became a better person. I am so sorry that as a community we have not talked about this enough.

It is ok to get a mental health check-up. Depression is very real, though it is one of the most complex discussions that have several layers, I want you to know that it is ok to go and get help. Mental Health in the African American community and in many spiritual arenas is taboo and not talked about, but depression and other mental health challenges are real. I have experienced some really dark days in my life, but through it all, I was able to survive what caused others to end it all. Though I never had to receive help formally, I do want you to know that it is ok to go and get it. I was fortunate to have a very strong support system coupled with great spiritual influences. I can easily identify with how quickly a person can be in a state of complete hopelessness and not recover.

If you are reading this book and contemplating harming yourself or ending it all, please call someone. If you are not struggling in this area but you know of family and friends that are going through a mental health struggle call them, check on them, tell them you love them, tell them that you will walk with them through this storm. Tell them that they are valued, loved, and lastly please make a referral for them. Below are a few steps that you can do to assist yourself or a person who may be having mental health challenges:

1. Go to your local Emergency Room for an evaluation.
2. Go see a therapist or counselor.

3. Contact the Suicide Prevention Hotline 1-800-273-8255.

As a Master Level Social Worker and Pastor, I want to also encourage those that are in ministry to quickly develop a resource list for your congregation. It is wise counsel to develop partnerships and make referrals when individuals are going through a mental health crisis. It is my practice to **always** refer out so that members can get the appropriate help that they need beyond their spiritual needs.

I almost titled this chapter "Caged." There is nothing like finding forgiveness and setting yourself free. One of the hardest things I had to do was to forgive myself. I had unrealistic expectations of myself that almost drove me crazy. I thought that I had to be perfect or that I had to live up to some false expectations of my family. In actuality, my only responsibility was just to be. It sounds so simple, but that is all I had to do.

The Value of Repentance

The value of repentance plainly means, to turn; to do an about face; to remove or walk away from one's wrongful actions. It generally involves a commitment to personal change and the resolve to live a more responsible and accountable life to God. If you have never experienced the joy of repentance, then you are really missing out. I once thought that if you had done wrong and I had on many occasions, then that sin or issue would follow you for the rest of your life. I must admit that once I got a good understanding of what true repentance was, then I positioned myself to live.

I will never forget the day I fully got the understanding of repentance; I was at my mother's funeral. My current pastor was speaking about how God will not hold sin against you if you repent. It was like a light bulb went off and while I was sitting there in the midst of all of my grief, God began to remind me that He would forgive me of pre-marital sex, lying, manipulation, smoking and drinking, the misuse of people in my life, and most importantly me denying who He called me to be. I knew that I had a purpose, but I denied it because I thought that I was too messed up, used up or too raggedy to be forgiven and it was at that moment that I began to repent and asked God to forgive me. The beautiful thing about repentance is that once you do it, it gets easier and easier. Think about it; God knows everything anyway.

He is everywhere so you really cannot hide anything from Him. He just wants you to come clean with Him. We must understand these three things about God.

- **God is omnipotent.** This means God is all-powerful. He spoke all things into being, and He sustains every cell, every breath, and every thought. There is nothing too difficult for Him to do *(Jeremiah 32:17-18, 26-27.)*

- **God is omniscient.** This means God is all-knowing. God's knowledge encompasses every possible thing that exists, has ever existed, or will ever exist. Nothing is a mystery or surprise to Him (Psalm 139:1-6).

- **God is omnipresent**. God is everywhere. He is in everything; around everything and close to everyone. "'Do not I fill heaven and earth?' declares the Lord" (Psalm 139:7-12).

Clean Out Your Backpack

What is it that you need to come clean about? What mistake has you caged? It is my hope that you take time today to do what I did and clean out your backpack. Oftentimes, we carry so many things in this life that they begin to weigh us down. I know what it is like to carry baggage. I know what it is like to carry sin, and I know what it is like to carry things from my past.

For example, what past failures or struggles seem to continuously show up in your life that you need to get rid of today? My oldest son does this thing in school where he goes through his classes, and he never cleans out his backpack. Typically, it is full of old grades, past write-ups, and old material that one does not need anymore. He misses the deadline on some things just because his backpack was full and was not organized. We do the same thing in life. Sometimes, we carry things for years that we do not need, and after a while, it becomes a hindrance to where we are going. You can't get to the next level because your backpack is full.

Take time to reevaluate your past and deal with those unresolved issues. Press toward the goal to win the prize for which God has called us. I encourage you to sort through your old papers, throw away the old snacks, and simplify your materials so that when something is needed, you will not miss the deadlines. Also, be sure to throw away those old letters that may be in the secret part of the backpack, which is evidence that you are holding on to some things in your past. Your backpack should only have the supplies that you need for the next class (journey) that you are about to enter. So, drop the unneeded weight, repent and keep it moving. Your destiny is waiting for you.

Chapter Six
I Am Free

Benjamin Chives explained that change does not roll in on the wheels of inevitability, but comes through continuous struggle. Therefore, we must straighten our backs and work for our freedom. Martin Luther King, Jr. said, "A man can't ride you unless your back is bent." Have you ever just sat back and looked at how far you have come? My life has not always been pretty, but I am grateful for the newfound freedom that I am living in. One of the struggles that I have noticed is that several people are free, but refuse to be grateful for the freedom. Let me make it plain. I believe that freedom is the ability to live your life knowing that you have not been perfect. Knowing that you have flaws, but serve a God who is able to perfect you is the greatest freedom of all. You do not have to be ashamed of your past, but you must embrace your future. Now let me be very clear, I am not speaking about sharing your testimony before deliverance has taken place. Oftentimes, people are so quick to share their struggles when they have not embraced freedom or have not been fully delivered.

In my opinion, sharing before deliverance has taken place is a very dangerous thing. People often attempt to build platforms off their struggles when they have not completely walked out their deliverance. When this occurs, they are setting themselves up to attract familiar spirits. Though I will not speak much in this book about familiar spirits, I would release the encouragement to be cautious of temporary freedom.

You need to be totally free so that you can assist others. Recently I read a post, and I am unsure of the author, but they stated something to the fact that you cannot get well in the same environment that you got sick in. Remember, that you need a sterile place so that your freedom can be perfected. I am all about sharing, but please be careful because everyone cannot handle your story. I believe if we master this lesson, we can really protect our freedom.

Locate your safe place (a place where you can be vulnerable and honest).

I AM SOMEBODY

_____
_____
_____
_____
_____
_____
_____
_____
_____
_____

Describe what freedom looks and feels like to you.

_____
_____
_____
_____
_____
_____
_____

Chapter Seven
I Am a Dreamer

Ask Joseph... sometimes your cloak of favor (coat of many colors) will attract the adversary, but don't let that throw you off. They can take your outside garment, but they can't take your favor. You were chosen for this.
Willie Diggs

The story of Joseph is one of those stories that have inspired me through this journey of discovering that *I Am Somebody*. Many times, our imagination or visions of who we are is a tool that God uses most times to address us. God has a way of painting us pictures and allowing us to see the very thing that we are designed to be without seeing the pits along the way. I often have wondered why God did not show us our pit experiences, but as I have matured, I have become comfortable with trusting his plans for my eyes. For me, if He had shown me the whole thing in the beginning, you would not be reading this book. I would have quit trying to make it a long time ago. Nevertheless, it was because of the dreams that God has giving me that I know without a doubt I am supposed to be here. Take this journey with me through this chapter as we look at how the ability to persevere and withstand the tests of life will produce destiny. As the quote explained, the favor that is on your life will attract the adversary, and there are times the people who are closet to you will be used by him. Let the attacks be an encouragement to you that you are somebody!

The Beginning Story of the Dreamer

Genesis 37:8-13 (NLT)

8 His brothers responded, "So you think you will be our king, do you? Do you actually think you will reign over us?" And they hated him all the more because of his dreams and the way he talked about them. 9 Soon Joseph had another dream, and again he told his brothers about it. "Listen, I have had another dream," he said. "The sun, moon, and eleven stars bowed low before me!" 10 This time he told the dream to his father as well as to his brothers, but his father scolded him. "What kind of dream is that?" he asked. "Will your mother and I and your brothers actually come and bow to the ground before you?" **11** But while his brothers were jealous of Joseph, his father wondered what the dreams meant. **12** Soon after this, Joseph's brothers went to pasture their father's flocks at Shechem. **13** When they had been gone for some time, Jacob said to Joseph, "Your brothers are pasturing the sheep at Shechem. Get ready, and I will send you to them."

Genesis 37:18-20 (NLT)

18 When Joseph's brothers saw him coming, they recognized him in the distance. As he approached, they made plans to kill him. **19** "Here comes the dreamer!" they said. **20** "Come on, let's kill him and throw him into one of these cisterns. We can tell our father, 'A wild animal has eaten him.' Then we'll see what becomes of his dreams!"

The Holy Spirit instructed me to speak to three types of people. These people are:

1. **The Survivor** (when there is a hit out on you because of the father's favor).

2. **The Dreamer** (the person who God has given a

huge vision of their life, but the situations don't add up).

3. **The Gifted** in waiting. (These people are extremely talented but are in a waiting period before what they saw manifest

The Survivor

A survivor is an individual who continues to live in spite of circumstances that would have killed others. Our story, which is much like Joseph, is a tale of many survival struggles and victories. We all have come through some very difficult times and if we continue on this journey destiny will show up.

The story of Joseph is one of my favorites because it deals with a young man who is favored by his father and because the father loved him so much, he gave him a coat of many colors. I believe this coat is symbolic of the outward appearance of your favor. An interesting fact is that even before Joseph could really enjoy the favor on his life he shared with some of his brothers a dream that he had. The dream showcased Joseph's brothers bowing to him. I would say that we are similar to Joseph. When God shows us these amazing dreams, we want to quickly tell others about them. I will not focus so much on the fact that because he shared his dreams that his brothers hated him. I want to put more emphasis on the fact that because of his dream he was able to survive the attacks. Because of the favor of God, he survived the pit that his brothers put him in; he survived the lies that were told by Potiphar's wife, and he survived the prison. His story is one of a survivor and the ability to overcome. One of the main reasons I like this story is that he did not allow the struggles of his past to cause him to abandon his dream.

What have you survived? Write them down as a reference point and read them to yourself when the whispers of the enemy get loud. Writing them down also allows you the opportunity to view how faithful God has been to you because of the dream he has given you.

I survived....

_____

_____

I AM SOMEBODY

_____
_____
_____
_____
_____
_____
_____
_____
_____
_____
_____
_____
_____
_____
_____
_____
_____
_____
_____
_____

The Dreamer

There is a dreamer in all of us. Even as kids, we had big imaginations and people often called us dramatic, daydreamers, or drama people. The story of Joseph and his dream is as exciting as they come. The idea that many of us will be something bigger than most people could imagine is not only frightening to the onlooker but is even more frightening to those who have the dream. Many times people will make you feel like your dream is too big. I believe that many of us will never walk in what we have dreamed because of the attacks that come based on what we shared. Do not mute your dream simply because people do not support you or because of the warfare that sometimes goes along with it.

I think that it was Joseph's belief in his dream that allowed him to survive all of the struggles of his life journey. I further believe that because he did not give in to the struggle and allow his trials to cause him to doubt what he saw that he was able to stay focused. When you have big dreams, it will take laser-like focus to stay on task. Many of us would throw in the towel or quit just because people are talking about us. Joseph did not allow his current situations to make him doubt what he saw. I have a question for you; do you believe what you saw? Do you believe that the Lord of all creation has favored you in such a way that everything in you will meet destiny? Do you believe that God will not show you anything that you cannot achieve if you stay the course? I want to encourage you today to dream and keep on dreaming.

We are a group of highly favored people who have been given big imaginations, and we should not lower them because of what we are going through. I often tell people when I am speaking that you are not your storm, meaning you are not the struggles and the accusations that people usually try to put on you. You are a part of the sonship of God, and you have a purpose and a destiny that is calling you very loud. I need you to make it; your family needs you to make it; your school and friends need you to make it; your church needs you to make it, and your children need you to make. Joseph, dust yourself off; the palace is calling you?

What do you see when you dream? What vision has God given you that warfare has made you doubt? Write your vision down.

_____
_____
_____

I AM SOMEBODY

_____
_____
_____
_____
_____
_____
_____
_____
_____
_____
_____
_____
_____
_____
_____
_____

I think that it is important to write what you see. Life will sometimes paint dreamers different pictures. For example, as a kid, I could see myself writing books and speaking to people. Although many, many years later, I am doing just what I saw, life painted a different picture. I had speech difficulties and issues with confidence. I often look at my children, and I see how quickly I could have quit and removed the examples of greatness from their reach. I want them to see me be everything that God said and showed me that I could be. I want them to see me publishing books, doing research, completing lectures, helping people, and being who God said I was. I want them to see what perseverance looks like so that if there is any doubt in their minds of who they are and what they can become they will look at their father and see my life as an example.

The Gifted in Waiting

The gifted in waiting is an individual who is extremely talented but needs the anointing. It was Joseph's pressing experiences that made him anointed. The one thing you can respect about dreamers is that those who hold on to the dream, survive the struggles, and remain faithful to the process come out anointed and powerful. Joseph was not just gifted but also anointed and faithful. Your character will surely be tested throughout the struggles of life. If Joseph had only been gifted, he would have saved the sharing of his gifting for the masses. However, he was faithful over his small assignments, and that is what makes him memorable. The many gifts that Joseph had, coupled with the struggles, could have caused him to be negligent of his dream and gifts. He was open to using his gifts no matter where his physical location may have been. He used his gifts in Potiphar's house, which allowed him to lead Potiphar's business with integrity. This is how we know that struggles produced character. When Joseph could have allowed the pressures of Potiphar's wife to make him lose his character, his integrity remained intact, he remained faithful to the assignment and focused on the dream God had given him.

Joseph's story provides us with a gold mine for the gifted and waiting. Joseph's family was very dysfunctional, such as many of ours. Your family history does not disqualify you from being a dreamer. I would say that your dysfunction probably allows you to be more open to dreams. Jacob and Rachel were Joseph's parents. They both had locked in their DNA the ability to wait. Both were coupled with dysfunction and what appeared to be broken promises. However, their ability to wait and remain focused on the promise proved to be a blessing for them. Jacob fell in love with Rachel and was required to work for her father Laban for seven years before he could marry her. Laban was a trickster, and after the seven years were up, he replaced Rachel with Leah, who was the oldest sister. Instead of Jacob marrying the one he loved and adored, he spent his wedding night with her sister Leah. Because he loved and admired Rachel so much Jacob agreed to work another seven years before he could be united with her.

Do you see the dysfunction? Do you see what appeared to be a broken promise? Jacob was a persistent brother, so instead of giving up on her, he agreed to work another seven years, which made it a total of fourteen years that he worked for Laban before he could marry Rachel. She had to be bad!!!!! Now I wish I could tell you that was the end of the struggle, but Rachel who wanted to have children, was unable to conceive and for many years suffered. There is a message in that. The message is that when it is time, the dream and desire will match and the baby will be born. That is how we get the story of the dreamer. One major takeaway from this story is that although there was dysfunction in Joseph's bloodline, his parents had the ability to hold on to the promises and visions of God and wait for them to manifest. My challenge to you is to keep working while you wait; keep learning while you wait; keep believing while you wait, and your dream will eventually show up. He did not allow the temporary circumstances of life to cause him to forfeit his dream. He was also willing to wait until it was time. Joseph is a perfect example of the gifted and waiting.

What are some things that you can do while you wait? I will give you three examples to review.

Self-Development

Research and list below the books you are currently reading or can read and the workshops you plan on attending.

_____
_____
_____
_____
_____
_____

I AM SOMEBODY

Chapter Eight
I Am a Father/Mentor

One of the greatest joys of my life is that of a father and mentor
Willie Diggs

My children and grandchildren are very special to me. While I must admit that when I became a father, I was unaware of what I was doing. They have proven to be one of the most influential parts of my development. I want to take time in this chapter to discuss what happens when a father is not in place. Many times, our children are searching for who they are like. I did the same thing because of the absence of the male role model. I often look at my children, and I see the life, confidence, and intelligence that they have all because I am present.

I wish I could tell you that I have done everything perfectly, but that would not be a true statement. I have made many mistakes with raising my children. If you asked them, they would tell you that I am quick to ask for forgiveness. I think that is very important that fathers provide our children with the opportunities to look at our model and see that even when mistakes occur, we should always ask for forgiveness. Fathers, take time today to affirm your children. Even if you are not living with them, send a text, or phone call. Do whatever it takes for them to understand that you value who they are. I make a commitment to my children to always affirm who they are. Below is a short list of words that you can use to affirm your children, friends, nieces, nephews, and mentees.

- I love you!
- You are awesome!
- I am proud of you!
- You are a world changer!
- You are beautiful!
- You are smart!
- You are God's child!
- You make me smile!
- The favor of God is on your life!
- I believe in you!
- I will always be with you!

Scriptural Affirmations

Isaiah 40:30-31 (NIV)

30 Even youth grow tired and weary,
 and young men stumble and fall;
31 but those who hope in the LORD
 will renew their strength.
They will soar on wings like eagles;
 they will run and not grow weary,
 they will walk and not be faint.

Philippians 4:13 (NIV)

13 I can do all this through him who gives me strength.

Jeremiah 1:5 (NIV)

5 "Before I formed you in the womb I knew you, before you were born I set you apart; I appointed you as a prophet to the nations."

Mentoring

I started mentoring when I was 19 years old. When I started, I had no idea that twenty years later I would be doing the same thing. My mentees, who I affectionately call my sons and daughters range in age and occupations. One of my goals as a mentor is to make sure that they always have support and encouragement. I am blessed to have had some great mentors who saw something in me that I did not see in myself or was too afraid to accept.

The Day I met Kim Womack (Social Worker)

One day while I was an undergraduate student, I walked into the office of Kim Womack, who happened to be a social work instructor at Jacksonville State University. I went into her office after deciding that I would change my major from music education to social work. I had just had a confrontation with a fraternity brother who made me get out of my bed and go get myself together. It is so important to have friends who will challenge you. So, I went into Kim's office with a load of issues. I was soon to be married, I was recovering academically, I had not met with an advisor for over a year, and I was all over the place. Luckily, Kim was a good listener and challenged me to address my goals and stay focused. She was very patient with me, but most importantly, she saw something in me that I did not see in myself. After allowing her to guide me in my academic curriculum, I was able to finish my academic goal. She literally coached me to getting my first degree. It is my prayer and hope that I use Kim's willingness to listen, her ability to coach those that are all over the place, and her skillful approach to help those who desire help arrive at the place that God has called them to be. Every mentee needs a Kim.

It is so important that at some point in our lives that we find ourselves a mentor and be a mentor to someone who needs help. Whether you mentor formally or informally, it is important that you take as many people that grace will allow you to, under your wings and help them.

I formally started mentoring in the city of Huntsville around 2011 after I had a student to get murdered. His death made me feel so guilty. It was not because I did not offer him help, or even try to teach him a better way, but because in my heart, I knew that there was more that I should be doing. So, to all of the mentors across the world, know that my team and I are praying for you. I know how hard it is sometimes to find funding for activities and other like-minded individuals who will be able to encourage you. I hope that this book is a resource that you and your mentees can use to help meet your agreed upon goals. When you discover that you are somebody, you are able to help all of those who may be in the discovery phase of learning who they are. Mentors are one of the tools that I believe God uses to help us along the way.

Chapter Nine

An Open Letter to Fatherless Children

Dear Beloved,

    I am writing this letter to you because I literally understand the struggle of growing up without your dad. I lived it, so I know the silent thoughts, the many questions, and the damaging internal dialogue that you have had with yourself. I want to take the time to write you because I understand that your biological father may never have the courage to say these things to you.

    First, I want you to know that you are not an accident, a mistake, or a throwaway. Today, I want to take the time to help remove the pressure of trying to be like someone you do not know. It is ok to remove the mask and take a moment to cry if you need to because your father was not present. I know that you may have put these thoughts in the back of your mind, but as a person who has lived this, it will show up if you do not deal with it. I want to give you permission to be upset with your father for leaving you, but I also want to give you permission to move on. Please understand that the world is happy that you are here.

Next, I want to let you know that you have a purpose and a destiny. Yes, you have a destiny, this is just a part of your story, and you can survive it. I am a witness that you can make it. I want you to be your best, and I want you to grow and blossom into all that you can be. I hope that you remember that you are fearfully and wonderfully made and full of greatness.

Lastly, I want you to know that you are somebody. You have everything that the greats have, and you are a designer's original. Understand that you are supposed to be here. I want to take time to apologize for your dad not being around. I am sorry that we have allowed society to put you in a space that is not healthy. Today, I promise you that I will do everything in my power to get fathers back into the homes and help rectify the disparities that plague our youth.

I AM SOMEBODY

I promise to teach, mentor, coach, love, affirm, correct, and educate as many people that the Lord will allow. I want to end this letter by letting you know that I love you; I believe in you; and that YOU ARE SOMEBODY!!!!

Sincerely,

Willie F. Diggs II

CHAPTER TEN
I Am Somebody

Preparation is key to moving from one level to the next
Grover Pickett

When I was a young man, I often wondered how I would make it. One of the greatest lessons that I learned from my grandfathers was that you could always make your next day better if you prepared for it. In my life, I have had the opportunity to learn from many great people. Although life for me was difficult, I must admit that if it had not been for some jewels along the way, I would not be here. So, in closing this book, I want to share what these jewels have taught me with hopes that they will be a blessing to you. In getting to this place in my life and understanding that *I Am Somebody*, two individuals stood in the gap and loved on me. My granddads, Henry Diggs, and Grover Pickett, helped inspire me to learn and to grow. These men often played the background with little are no recognition, but I am the fruit of many small talks and lessons shared on their porch. They were great men of honor, courage, and dignity. They were fathers to their generations and left great seeds for me.

My grandfather Henry Diggs was a man of very few words. However, his love spoke often in the way he dealt with me. We often had long conversations on the porch about the simple things in life. He was a farmer, so he taught me the importance of sowing good seeds and how to take care of the things that you have planted. He also was a man who loved food, as I do! We often spent times eating and just talking about things that mattered to me like spiders, pigs, and jokes. He always had time to just talk and listen, which I think is the greatest lesson that I learned from him. No matter how busy life gets, always take time to talk to the people who matter to you. I often do this with my children and mentees as we spend several hours just talking, laughing, and being silly.

I tip my hat to the man who I get my features, my loving heart, ability to plant, and how to enjoy life. Granddad Henry often played the background, however; he was a forerunner to me. Thanks for being a humble man who did not judge, but loved. Let this short tribute bring honor to the man who I called Granddad and be a blessing to all who read this book. He was instrumental in helping me to understand that I AM SOMEBODY and YOU ARE TOO!

2 Corinthians 9:6 (GWT)
Remember this: The farmer who plants a few seeds will have a very small harvest. But the farmer who plants because he has received God's blessings will receive a harvest of God's blessings in return.

My grandfather Grover Pickett and I were very close. He was what I termed as the community's grandfather. He was a picture of a servant leader. He was a very mild tempered man who loved his family. He is the one who gave me the nickname "Buddy" which made me feel special. It allowed me to feel like I was very important to him. He too was a farmer and worked really hard to take care of his family. Because he was always so quick to help others, that trait runs through all of our family. Till this day my kids and I all continue to volunteer in the community. In his later years, he was the babysitter for my boys. I can remember how he would spend several hours loving on my children because he knew that they did not have a grandfather because my father was deceased. He would take my baby boy walking every day in his wagon. The love he shared for people is a model that I will follow. He never missed an opportunity to help or encourage someone who may be struggling.

I honor the man who loved me during a time when I thought I was unlovable, who cared for me when I was too immature to recognize that I even needed help, and took time to show me what true fatherhood looked like. My grandfather was a true model of the love of God.

It is my hope that after reading this book that you get the understanding that you are somebody. Life is not easy, but please believe that everything that you have been through can be used to push you into destiny. You are the answer to the world's questions; you are what is needed to help the world be great; you are indeed a designer's original who is fearfully and wonderfully made. You are the answer, and you are SOMEBODY!

I AM SOMEBODY

I always tell myself these four things before I go to bed. I encourage you to write them down. Post them on your mirror or door so that you can be reminded daily:

1. I love who I am!

2. I am better than I thought.

3. I can change the world!

4. I AM SOMEBODY!

I AM SOMEBODY

Willie F. Diggs II, LBSW, MSW

Known as a spiritual life coach for students, Willie Diggs is a motivational mentor who enjoys engaging students in a life dialogue of discovering who they are. Known for his passion to captivate individuals through small talk he continues to encourage people through academics, professionalism, and spirituality to become leaders in their community.

Willie is a native of Brundidge, Alabama. He currently serves as the Campus Pastor of the Beacon Butler Campus, Huntsville, AL the first church planted under Superintendent Anthony Wheeler. Sharing a strong passion and a burden to see individuals come to a life-altering encounter with the one who gave them life; Pastor Willie continues to spend countless hours mentoring and coaching individuals to become who God has called them to be.

Known for his creative approach to teaching, he continues to captivate individuals by drawing them into the scriptures and assisting them with a life dialogue of learning about the creator. Having worked with several populations, age groups, and cultures in the social service realm, he and his wife share a strong passion with educating the community and helping people deal with the many social issues that are plaguing our world. He is a preacher, motivational speaker, spiritual life coach, teacher, author, and friend to many.

Willie is a Licensed Elder through the Church of God in Christ. Educated at Jacksonville State University where he graduated with a Bachelor of Social Work Degree and later graduated from Alabama A&M where he received a Masters of Social Work Degree and now serves as an Assistant Instructor and Director of Field Education.

He is a workshop speaker, parent educator, and resource builder in his community. He is the founder of Come Thirsty Ministries, Inc., a non-profit organization that develops Christ centered programs to assist people with changing their lives and the world. The programs include Focus on the Future Mentor Program, Restore Me Community Health Fair, God's Girls Rock Program, and Come Thirsty Kids Program.

He was born to the late Staff Sgt. Willie F. Diggs and Carolyn Diggs of Brundidge, Alabama. He is a member of Phi Beta Sigma Fraternity, Inc. and the 100 Black Men of America. He is married to his loving wife Shataun Diggs and is the father of 3 young boys.

Facebook: willie.diggs.5 | Twitter: @IamWillieDiggs @ComeThirstyMin | Instagram: @IamWillieDiggs

For booking please call 256-225-9384 or email jabas03@aol.com